Copyrighted Material

This book or parts thereof may not be reproduced in any form whatsoever, store or transmitted by any means- electronic, photocopy, mechanical recording or otherwise without prior permission of the publisher.

Copyright @2020 by Walter Abraham

All right reserved

Table of contents

Introduction	3
What is a bond?	4
Bonds terminology you need to know	4
Investing basic: Bonds	12
The bond market	17
The bond market cycle	24
How do I make money buying bonds?	26
Guaranteed Investment Certificate	27
Benefits of investing in equity, debt and liquid instruments	34
Equity	34
Debts instruments	36
Liquid assets	38
Balance fund	38
Bonds prices and interest rates	40
Period	43

INTRODUCTION:
Sometimes, when we mentioned the word "debt" what readily comes to mind is the credit cards and loans. This may be right but debts entails more than this. The dictionary definition of debt is money that is owed.

Bonds are also known as debts or fixed income and can be further categorized into two i.e. as either good or bad debts. Good debts on one side are investment that create tangible values, example of such investment are student loan and mortgage. On the other hand, bad debts are money owed to creditors and unlikely to be paid. In other words, bad debt is a portion of a loan portfolio a lender considers to be uncollectable. It is known as high-interest consumer debt in personal finance. Examples of bad bets are; car loan, store credit card or credit card.

What is a bond?

A bond can simply be described as a borrowing agreement between two parties (i.e. the issuer of the bond and the purchaser of the bond), where the bond issuer promises to pay the bond purchaser a specify amount of money at a specify interest rate after certain period of time.

Bonds Terminology

Bonds trading are associated with terminologies which are often used in the market. As a new entrant in this market, it's important to you understand these terminologies. Some of the key bond terms are;

1- Par Value

This is the amount returned to the investor at bond maturity, it is also known as the face value of the bond. Suppose the bond was issue for $1,000 and an investor bought it at that price i.e. the bond was bought at its par value. The investor will equally get back his $1,000 back at maturity date. The Bond par value is mostly at $1,000, though there are exceptions sometimes.

2- Discount

Bonds can be trade above or below their original par value. Since bond per value is mostly trading at $1,000, any bond trading below $1,000 is trading at a discount.

3- Premium

This is the direct opposite of a discount trade. This means that bonds are trading above the par value i.e. more than

$1,000. For instance, a bond trading at $1,050.25 is said to be trading at $50.25 premium per bond.

4- Coupon Interest Rate

This is the interest rate of the bond. Some bonds pay interest twice a year. Furthermore, some bonds have floating or adjustable interest rates which are subject to certain indices. The implication of this is that the coupon payment will fluctuate based on the underlying indices.

5- Maturity

Every bond has a lifetime and that lifetime can last anywhere from one month to 50 years. Bonds maturity is the period when the bond becomes due for payment i.e. the expiration of the bond contract when the bondholder receives the par value of the bond. The maturity period for the medium-term bonds is usually between one to ten years, while the long term bonds maturity is mostly ten years or longer.

6- Market Rates of Interest

This is the prevailing interest rate of bonds in the market, the interest rate fluctuates and the market rates of interest greatly affect bond prices.

For example, suppose a coupon rate of bond you bought last year was 5% and the market interest rates as at that time was also 5% and you paid $1,000 for each bond. Now, the market interest rates have risen to 6% this year. The question is, if you tried to sell this bond at the moment, what price would you get?

It is obvious that a buyer would not pay the same $1,000 per bond for a 5% interest yielding bonds when the buyer has an alternative of buying a new $1,000 bonds with 6% current coupon rates. This indicates that this bond will end up selling at a discount in order to stand a chance of being competitive with the current bonds in the market.

The same law is applicable to a situation where market rates fall below the coupon rate. The investor will have to buy the bond at a premium by paying more.

7- Call Provision

This is when bonds issuer call or redeem the bonds before their maturity at a specified price. Bonds issuer can exercise the call provision when face with unfavorable market e.g. when interest fall below the coupon rate of the bonds. This allows them to issue new bonds at a lower rate of interest and this invariably costs them less interest payments to bonds investors.

8- Bid Price:

Bonds are usually quoted on a basis of bid and ask price. Bids price is the highest price buyers are ready to pay for bond in the market.

9- Ask Price:

This is the lowest price offered by sellers of the issue.

10-Spread:

The difference between the bid and the ask price is referred to as the spread. Portion of this is a commission that is earned by the broker or dealer. A large spread on a bond is a signal that the bonds are inactively traded.

11- Basis Point

This is used to measure the differences in bond yields and it can simply be explained as one hundredth of one percent point. Suppose bond yield falls from 5.25% to 5.20, this mean that the yield decline is five basis points.

12-Secured bonds

Secured bonds are bonds that are backed by collateral. The implication of this is that, the company issuing the bond must have money or assets to cover the value of the bonds. The assets would be given to the people who bought the bonds in case that the company goes bankrupt.

13-Unsecured bonds
These types of bonds are not backed by any collateral. Rather, they are simply covered by the creditworthiness or goodwill of the company issuing the bonds. Unsecured bond is also known as debentures. Example, most of the government bonds are unsecured because the government is credit worthy.

14- Callability: This is a term that means the company or agency that issued the bond has the right to call the bond back. In other words, the company buys the bond back before it matures. An agency might do this when interest rates are falling in order to issue new bonds at lower rates so it'll save money. This isn't always a bad deal for those who bought the bonds either, because there is an extra premium added to the face value of the bond.

This callability allows the seller to call the bond back before it matures. Some but not too many bonds have a part provision that gives the person who bought the bond a chance to sell it back at face value before it matures, it can't be done at any time. However, the seller must schedule this ahead of time. People who own bonds sometimes puts their bonds when interest rates are rising so they can invest their money where it will earn more convertible bonds.

Sometimes, bonds can be converted into stock in the company that issued them at the time. The convertible bonds are issued exactly when and at what price, they can be converted to stocks. This type of bond usually offers lower interest rates initially but it's also offers the potential for higher earnings as a stock secured bonds.

Investing Basics: Bonds

Bonds are popular investment in the capital market but they remain a mystery to many investors especially the beginners. So, as investors, how does a bond benefit your investment portfolio?

As we have mentioned earlier, a bond is a loan given to a company or government by an investor at a fixed interest rate over a period of time. In other words, company and government issue out bonds in order to attract investors to bring in capital to fund their ongoing projects or new projects. Investors on the other hand see opportunity in bonds as a way of preserving their money as well as generating additional income.

Bonds are considered as less risky compared to stocks and can be used to diversify investment portfolio. Let's look at this example. Suppose a company named boom decides to construct a new shopping mall and is ready to raise the capital for the project through bonds issuance at face value of $1,000. Each of the company's bond issued by the company is actually a loan in its book. Suppose the bond maturity period is ten years with a coupon rate or interest rate of 5%.

What this means is that the company will continue to pays the investors $50 on a yearly basis for ten years and once the bond reaches ten years agreed period, the investors his bond and the company returns his $1,000 principal capital investment. Thus, it's a win-win situation for both parties. The company got capital for its new construction and the investor equally got yearly interest payment for the bond period in addition to the returns of his principal capital invested in the bond.

Bonds are considered as stable and predictable form of investment because of its regular scheduled of its coupon rate of interest payment as well as returned of the invested principal at maturity. This is contrary to stocks investment where market forces are the determinant of profits and losses and are also less predictable. However, bonds equally have its own risk and one of such is the possibility of default in paying back the principal amount. This is called default risk and bonds with higher default risk often offer higher coupon rates. The amount of risk also depends on the financial capability of the bonds' issuer. Government bonds are considered to have less default risk because of its financial stability, though government bonds are often issue with low coupon rate.

Corporate organization can issue corporate bonds with higher coupon rate. The coupon rate being offer on some of these bonds may look tempting but investors especially beginners have to be careful because corporate bonds typically risk of default, as companies can go bankrupt and that would be the end of the principal capital invested. That's the basic reason behind higher coupon rates of corporate bonds.

To assist investors determine the financial capability of the bond issuer, rankings are being assigned by several credit rating agencies and these rating agencies employed different indices in measuring risk. So as a beginner, it's wise to always compare rating when considering a certain bond but note that rating agencies too are not always accurate. So it your primary responsibility to research a bond and its associated risk before you invest.

Interest rate is another risk worthy of consideration in bonds investment. This is the risk that your bonds would be worth less in value in a situation where interest rates goes up and you decide to sell before the maturity. It is a common thing to see more investors allocate their capital into new bonds that offer higher interest rates when the interest rates rise in the market. So as an investor, in order to dispose the low interest rate bond to buy the new high interest rates bonds, you have to sell your low interest rates bonds at a discount to make it attractive for another investor.

Bonds might be part of a diversified portfolio through two major ways i.e.

income generation and capital preservation. A lot of investors pursue their investment goals through the mix of stocks and bonds. This helps to safe guard and increase portfolio returns.

This section only deals with just a simple way investors can use bonds and few risks associated with bonds. Bonds are complex investment with associated risks just like every other investment. So it's necessary to research more before you invest in it.

The bond market

It is normal for individual who need to borrow money to approach financial intermediary like bank, but for a big brand like Apple, borrowing money may be available through other source i.e. the bond market.

Bonds are like an IOU which shows who owes what and when the repayment will be made. It is also traded on markets just like stocks. Well established company like Apple is already known by investors and they'll be willing to lend to the company directly. Thus, company like Apple may not necessary need a financial intermediary like bank to lend from. They can access loan on better terms through bond than they can through normal bank borrowing. This is equally applicable to so many large companies with a good reputation. For example, in order to fund new projects, Apple has issued more than a billion dollars of corporate bonds over the years.

One notable feature of bond as compare to stock is in the area of part-ownership of business. Unlike stocks where a stockholder automatically become part-owner of business, the bond does not confer you with privileges, you don't own part of the business. You are simply lending the business money and in exchange you will be paid a specific amount at a certain period of time.

Furthermore, some bonds pay out frequent installments known s coupon payments based on a pre-determined schedule. Company can raise the needed capital for further investments by issuing bond to investors. Though this bond constitutes a debt to the company but it can be repay over a long period of time as those investments provide a return.

Large corporations are not the only institutions that raise capital through the bond market, the government also do as well. For example, in 2016, the amount of money the U.S government owed the public in promised bond payments was about $14 trillion and this have effect on the entire market for saving and borrowing.

Let's look at the supply and demand for loanable funds with some numbers and simple graph for our illustration.

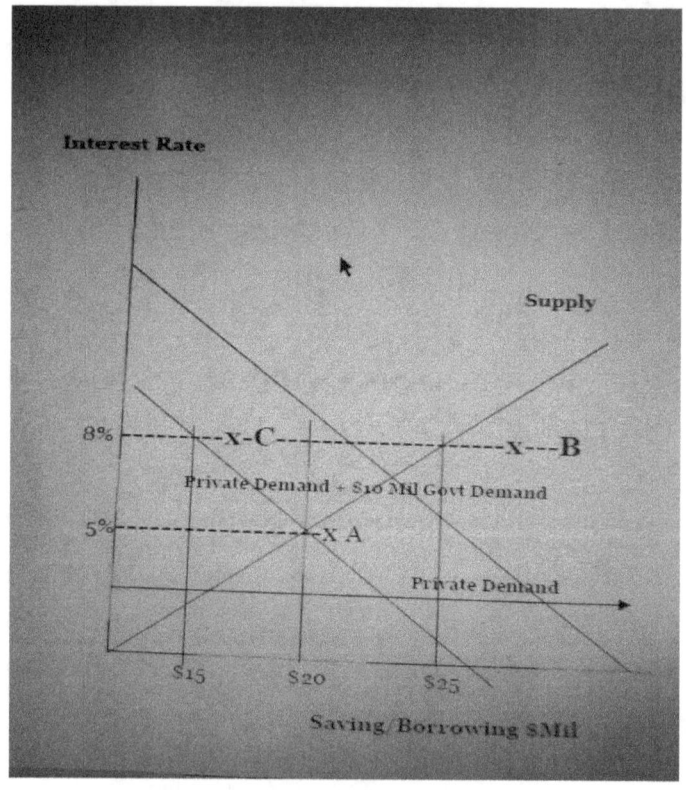

The demand curve above shows the demand for borrowing. Suppose that the government is ready to borrow $10

million. This will result to shifts in the demand for loanable funds upward and to the right thereby increasing the equilibrium interest rate from 5% to 8%.

At a higher interest rate, the quantity of savings supplied increases from $20 to $25 million. So, if savings increases by $5 million that means that private consumption is falling by $5 million. By saving more will also mean that we're consuming less. And this will make private investment to fall since it has become much more expensive to borrow as a result of the higher interest rate.

The private demand for loanable fund at 8% stand at $15million which was $5 million less than lower than it was when the interest rate was 5%. These two effects are referred to as "crowding out". When the government borrows $10 million, private consumption and private investment are crowded out. In this scenario, $5 million of private consumption and 5$ million of private investment are crowded out.

Bonds are less risky to stocks because the bondholders get paid first before any profits are shared to the shareholders. Like it was mentioned in earlier, bonds do have associated risk. The main risk is the default risk- meaning that when the payments come due, the company may not be able to pay the bondholders. Investors on their part usually demand higher interest rate if they think that a firm issuing a bond has a significant default risk.

Bonds are being rated by agency like S&P and these ratings are from AAA down to D. AAA rating is the safest bonds and any rating lower than BBB- are called junk bonds. Apple for example has a rating of AA+ which is pretty safe to lend to.

It must be reiterated that rating agencies are not always perfect as was witnessed during the recent financial crisis where some highly rated bonds failed to live up to the market expectation . However, higher rated bonds pay lower interest rates because they are consider safer while lower rated bonds because of their risky nature pay higher interest rates in order to attract investors who are willing and ready to take risk.

In the whole of United States, the lowest bond rating of any state government can be found in the state of Illinois. It has an average of A- which means that it has to borrow more unlike the state of Virginia with AAA rating, the highest in the United States.

The ability of the borrower to put up collateral is another factor that determines the interest rate on bond. The collateral can be in form of asset that helps to guarantee the loan in an event of unforeseen circumstances. So the logic is that you will typically get a lower interest rate if you want to borrow money to buy a house and a higher interest rate if it is for a vacation.

The vacation loan is more risky to the bank than the mortgage loan because in case of default, the vacation can't be repossess once you have enjoyed it but house can be repossess because it is the collateral for the loan. So it's far cheaper and easier to borrow money to buy a house than to go on vacation.

The bond market cycle

The bond market play a leading role in any economy of the world as it's mostly bigger than the stock market. For example, in the US as at the year 2016, the amount invested in the bond market was $39 trillion compare to the stock market that had just $29 trillion.

The bond market comprises of issuers like the federal government, municipalities and corporations waiting to lend capital from investors. These capital borrowed from investors are use for many purpose. For example, the money can be use for infrastructure development like roads construction by the federal government.

Capital can be raised by city or town by issuing municipal bonds and capital realized can be channel to fund local projects like construction or building of city hall, new schools or airport. Corporations may equally issue bonds for various reasons. Corporations can issue bonds to raise capital in order to complete ongoing projects or to embark on new projects.

For example, a construction can raise money through bond to finance an expansion project. This expansion project could have a positive impact on the overall economy in many ways. The expansion would create new jobs that would provide paychecks to new employees. The new employees could spend or invest their earnings in the economy and this further boost the economy. This type of transaction happens daily and it creates a positive cycle good for the economy growth. Remember, this began with just a bond transaction between an issuer an investor before it trickle down the line. The issuer raises the capital to finance and execute his projects while the investor benefits by receiving interest on the capital invested.

How do I make money buying bonds?

Investors can make money in capital market by providing capital for companies to use for their business growth and in turn get paid an agreed interest rate. Investors can either invest in either company stocks (shares) or bonds (debt). In actual sense, what you make as a return on your investments is largely depends on what you are investing in. Among the various investments options available to investors are;

a- Guaranteed Investment Certificate (GIC):

Guaranteed Investment Certificate (GIC) is the easiest type of fixed income. The unique thing about this type of deposits is that as the name suggested, it's guaranteed up to a certain amount of the investment. Suppose you hold a GIC of a company and you are under the limit when the value goes up, you are not at risk of losing your initial investment or interest.

There is always a specified interest rate for a Guaranteed Investment Certificate (GIC). Suppose a 5 years Guaranteed Investment Certificate with an interest of 3% was purchased by an investor. For each of those 5 years period, the investor will get 3% guaranteed interest rate payment, and the initial investment will be returned after 5 years.

The Guaranteed Investment Certificate has different interest payment frequency. The Guaranteed Investment Certificate interest payment frequency can be monthly or yearly. In some cases, the interest can simply be reinvested back to the business on yearly basis and the cumulative interest paid together with the principal at the maturity of the Guaranteed Investment Certificate.

Most Guaranteed Investment Certificate have locked-in feature where you don't have access to your money till the Guaranteed Investment Certificate matures. In a case where you are granted access, you are likely to forfeit all interest the investment must have accumulated. It is important to state that there is cashable Guaranteed Investment Certificate that allows you to make withdrawal with 30 or 60 days prior notice but this form of Guaranteed Investment Certificate often pays a lower interest rate.

b- Bonds:
Bond is the second type of investment option available to investors. As we have mentioned earlier, bonds gives investor opportunity to lend capital to a corporation or government for certain period of time at a fixed interest rates i.e. investors keeps earning interest on the bond on yearly basis and upon the maturity of the bond, the investor's initial principal amount is returned.

Suppose I want to invest $10,000 in a corporate bond. The initial value of that bond which is the $10,000 is referred to as par value. So I will be getting an annual interest return of 4% twice a year for lending my money to company for use. This mean that I will be getting $200 every six months and that $200 is known as a coupon payment. Since the term on the bond is five years period, I will keep getting this coupon payment for five years and after five years, I'll get back my initial $10,000. This type of income is tagged interest income by the tax authority.

Sounds very easy right? Well it is easy ... if you have your $10,000 available when a company is issuing bonds (in other words, undergoing the procedure of collecting a chunk of cash from investors to invest in a project as well as setting out the borrowing regards to the bond- the interest rate, maturation date, and also a potential host of various other items not appropriate to this conversation).

But the truth is that companies do not do this each time they require $10,000. They'll issue a lot of bonds and also accumulate a big amount of money at the same time. This indicates that when you have your $10,000 prepared to spend, you effectively might not be buying a bond when the federal government or firm first problems it. You'll be buying it from other financiers who bought it when it was initially released. This indicates that depending upon what has actually occurred in markets given that the bond was released, the price could have changed.

For example, let's assume that the District of Ontario released that 4% interest bond in 2012. As we are aware that there have been significant dropped in oil prices and as well as interest rates in Canada. Coincidentally, a new bond that matures at the same period with that of 2012 was issued by the Province of Ontario, but as opposed to paying 4%, it's just paying 2.5% on it. If an investor can get that 4% bond, it would pay him better because that's an extra 1.5% annual interest rate for him!

To cover up for these higher interest rates, the markets adjust the cost of the bond so that you're in the same spot in term of returns if you had invested in the 4% coupon-paying bond or the 2.5% coupon-paying bond. The price of this bond might be around $110, implying that for each $100 worth of par value (what you'll get back at maturity), you would certainly pay $110. A bond that matures at $10,000 would cost you $11,000, however you're made up for that $1,000 loss by obtaining a greater interest rate along the road. This sort of bond is called a costs bond.

If on the other hand, interest rates increase, like it did recently for the very first time in 7 years, you would be hesitant to pay $10,000 for 4% paying bond, when you can as well purchase more extra bond for $10,000 that pays 5% instead! The market drives down the cost of the bonds to 4%, this is to motivate individuals to choose between the two bonds.

You possibly have to part with $9,500 for $10,000 worth of returns will still be received and, it will certainly just come from a various percentage of passion and funding gains. You'll get a reduced interest settlement on regular basis, and on maturity, you'll get an added $500. This kind of bond is known as a discount rate bond.

All points being equivalent, for investors that don't need to bother with tax (i.e. those who invest in RRSP's or TFSA's), ought to be indifferent between two bonds based upon their rates of interest, because they will be priced to provide you the specific same return.

In summary, when the prices of bonds fall, the interest rates will rise and when the prices rise the interest rates fall. Recall our previous discussion on the Guaranteed Investment Certificate (GIC). They are illiquid and they don't change in price like bonds do.

Benefits of investing in Equity, Debt and Liquid Instruments

In general, investment is simply the acts of buying and holding on to company's shares by individuals and firms in expectation of income from the dividend and the gain from the future rise in shares value of the company.

c. Equity:
Equities are highly rewarding investment among the available investment options. Though equities investments are very attractive to

investors because of its high rates of returns, its associated risks are equally high. Equity investment is like owning a small part of a business. Suppose a businessman need a capital of $10,000 to start a business. The businessman wants to channel this capital into acquisition of materials, retail outlet, labor and marketing activities. If an investor provides the said $10,000 capital needed for 50% stake in the business and the business grow over the years. The investor initial capital of $10,000 could equally multiply as the business grow in size and its value increase. Moreover, the investor may equally receive dividends from profits that are not plowed back to the business. Let remember that it's not all that rosy in the investment world, as the investor stand a risk of losing all or part of his capital investment if the business does not take off.

Equity mutual funds help an individual to reduce the risk of spending straight in equity for numerous factors. Fund supervisors are experts who have a lot more expertise of the markets than a typical financier does and also consequently their performance is likely to beat that of an average capitalist. Fund managers are trained to be money grubbing when others are frightened and also scared when others are greedy, consequently they are extra inclined than ordinary capitalists to cut losses when supplies do not execute well and also to include in their stock profile when others are selling and also prices are coming down. Most notably considering that equity mutual funds are expanded, the risk is spread over several stocks that instruments permit the debtor to increase funds at a certain rates of interest over a fixed time period.

DEBT INSTRUMENTS:

Sorts of financial obligation tools include; notes, bonds, home loans, leases or other contracts between a lender and also a customer. So if you purchase a financial obligation instrument, your resources is safeguarded and you recognize in advance what your financial investment will be worth over the moment period that you remain spent. There is little threat at the same time and the benefit is also limited or practically nil.

Debt instruments appropriate for those that have actually restricted threat taking capacity but at the same time would like to earn even more rate of interest on their resources than they would certainly by auto parking their money in banks financial debt. Mutual funds are among the methods where to buy financial debt tools your capital is protected since the kinds of bonds that fund managers choose to buy typically have high rankings therefore, the danger is therefore reduced as well as the return is modest. Mutual funds are the most tax effective kind of financial debt financial investment as compared to various other debt tools.

LIQUID ASSET:
A liquid possession is a possession that can be converted into cash money promptly. Fluid assets consist of most money market tools as well as government bonds. A fluid possession appropriates for those who need liquidity and also would likewise like to make interest on their funds while they are not being used. For fluid mutual funds rate of interest is payable also on bank holidays.

A liquid fund usually provides a greater rate of return than investments in various other comparable asset classes and also the return is tax obligation reliable.

BALANCED FUND:
In case you would like to have direct exposure to all the three types of financial investments discussed previously, a balanced fund could be the answer. A balanced fund typically has a supply element, a bond element as well as a cash market. One balanced funds are preferable for capitalists who are trying to find a mix of safety earnings and some resources recognition. Well balanced funds might have a high equity part for capitalists much more likely towards funding admiration and with some risk hunger or they may have a high financial obligation element for financiers more interested in revenue as well as protection.

Well balanced funds are a good idea for people with a lasting investment horizon. Your independent financial expert can help you select the instruments best fit for you, provided your needs and also run the risk of profile. Bear in mind, mutual fund financial investments are subject to market risks.

Bond Prices and Interest Rates

Bond costs and also rates of interest have an inverse connection. This implies that as interest rates increase in the economic climate bond costs will decrease and also as rates of interest fall in the economy bond prices will boost. The price of a bond refers to the principal or the stated value of a bond. For example, if you purchase a corporate bond for $5,000 the $5,000 you paid to acquire the bond is the rate of the bond it stands for the cash you provided to the corporation who issued the bond and considering that the $5,000 principal will be paid back when the bond becomes fully grown it additionally shows what the bond is job to the bond holder.

So, why are bond costs and also interest rates inverse? When an investor purchases a bond, the company of the bond consents to pay the capitalist an interest rate to obtain their cash this can impact the financiers' inspiration to buy the bond. For example allows presume that when you acquired the five thousand buck corporate bond, the company that sold you the bond consented to pay you 10% annually over the life of the bond. That rate of interest is secured and will certainly not alter which suggests you gain $500 in rate of interest every year guaranteed.

Currently, think that interest rates rise to 15% in the economic situation all brand-new bonds provided in the bond market will promptly earn capitalists much more revenue making the 10% passion on your bond less attractive therefore when you attempt to market your bond, investors will certainly walk away and buy a bond at the brand-new greater rates of interest. The only way that you can sell your bond is by lowering the rate to change for the difference in rate of interest, because of this the price of your bond will certainly lower to a reduced principal that is below the original $5,000 cost, but what if as opposed to rising to 15% interest rates are up to 5% in the economy. All brand-new bonds issued in the bond market will immediately make investors less earnings, making the 10% rate of interest on your bond extra eye-catching as a result if you attempt to offer your bond, capitalists will certainly be eager to bike due to the fact that your bond has a greater rate of interest than any kind of brand-new bonds.

To take advantage of the raised value of your bond, you'll change the principal for the distinction in rate of interest as a result of this. The rate of your bond will

boost a greater concept above the original $5,000 cost. It comes down to easy supply and also need when rates of interest increase your bond earns less profits at its fixed rate of interest that makes it less beneficial as well as much less demanded which decreases its cost. When rates of interest fall, your bond makes even more profit at its fixed interest rate which makes it more valuable and a lot more demanded and also
increase its price.

PERIOD
Duration is a measure of bonds interest rate sensitivity revealed in years. Typically the longer the duration the a lot more sensitive the bonds cost to interest rate changes and the higher the rate volatility it faces. On the other hand, shorter duration bonds are less sensitive to change in interest rate and it is subjected to lower price volatility.

There are three common kinds of duration and also reliable period is most typically made use of. Duration determines the moment it requires to settle the capitalist and also it is not equal to bond maturation. Duration is typically shorter than bond maturity, bonds pay promo code rate of interest along with maturation and voucher price.

Efficient duration additionally takes into account the embedded call features as well as yield to maturity. For example, if rates were to climb 1%, a bond profile with a duration of one decade would be anticipated to lose 10% by contrast a 1% price walking would create a profile with a period of 5 years to shed 5% of its worth. As a result, if rate of interest are anticipated to rise, a sensible technique would certainly be to hold bonds or mutual fund with shorter duration. The bond prices are much less sensitive to adjustments in rates of interest alternatively. It may make even more feeling to concentrate on longer duration bonds. Financiers must constantly be conscious about the market volatility as well as totally understand the investment dangers before proceeding further.